About This Book

Title: *Pushes and Pulls*

Step: 3

Word Count: 130

Skills in Focus: Digraph sh

Tricky Words: forces, make, move, away, sea, ball, toy, beach, too

Ideas For Using This Book

Before Reading:
- **Comprehension:** Look at the title and cover image together. Ask readers to think about a time when they have pushed or pulled something. What happened when they pushed or pulled?
- **Accuracy:** Practice saying the tricky words listed on page 1.
- **Phonemic Awareness:** Tell students they will read words with the digraph *sh*. Explain that a digraph is two letters that make one sound. Note that the /sh/ sound can be heard at the beginning or end of a word. Have readers listen as you segment the sounds in the word *push* (/p/, /u/, /sh/). Point out that the *u* in this word makes a slightly different sound than in a word like "pup." Ask readers to draw a dot with a marker for each sound they hear in the word *push*. Underline the dot that makes the /sh/ sound. Repeat with the word *dash*. Offer other examples that will appear in the book: *splash, crash, shell, shop, swish*.

During Reading:
- Have readers point under each word as they read it.
- **Decoding:** If readers are stuck on a word, help them say each sound and blend the sounds together smoothly. Be sure to point out any /sh/ digraph sounds.
- **Comprehension:** Invite students to talk about what new things they are learning about forces while reading. What are they learning that they didn't know before?

After Reading:
Discuss the book. Some ideas for questions:
- Pushes and pulls are types of forces. Where do you see these forces happening in the world around you?
- What do you still wonder about forces?

Pushes and Pulls

Text by Laura Stickney

Reading Consultant
Deborah MacPhee, PhD
Professor, School of Teaching and Learning
Illinois State University

PICTURE WINDOW BOOKS
a capstone imprint

Forces make things shift and move.

Pushes and pulls are forces.

A push shifts things away. Swish!

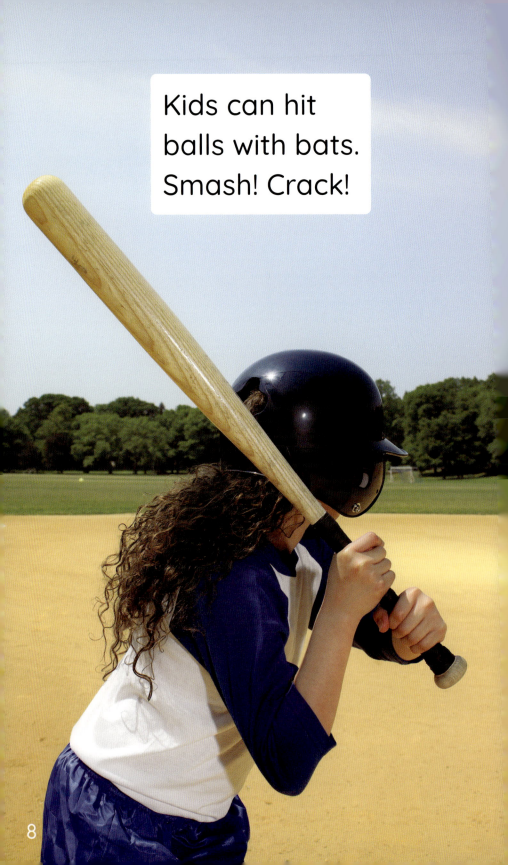
Kids can hit balls with bats. Smash! Crack!

This hit pushes a ball up and away.

Kids can push toy cars.
This makes the cars
rush as fast as a flash.

Pulls shift things too.

Dogs pull a sled.
The dogs dash fast.

At shops, pull dishes off a shelf. Put dishes in a cart. Then push the cart.

When you push the cart, it moves.

16

Do not crash it in the shop!

Rocks and shells sit still on sand.

Then the sea rushes
up to rocks and shells.

The sea swishes and sloshes. Crash!

It pulls shells and rocks in. Splash!

The sea can push rocks and shells onto the beach too.

More Ideas:

Phonics and Phonemic Awareness Activity

Practicing Digraph *sh*:
Play I Spy! Prepare word cards with *sh* story words. Place each card face up on a surface. Choose a word to start the game. Break apart the sounds and say, "I spy /p/, /u/, /sh/" or another word of your choice. The readers will call out the word, then look for the corresponding card. Continue until all cards have been collected. For an extra challenge, have students be the caller, choosing and breaking apart a word.

Suggested words: shifts, flash, dash, swish, splash, crash, slosh

Extended Learning Activity

Let's Experiment!
Ask readers to gather a few objects. Then ask them to make a prediction about what will happen to each object when it is pushed or pulled. Have readers conduct an experiment, observing what happens to each object when they push or pull it. After the experiment, have readers write a sentence about the results. Ask students to use words with *sh* in their sentences.

Published by Picture Window Books, an imprint of Capstone
1710 Roe Crest Drive, North Mankato, Minnesota 56003
capstonepub.com

Copyright © 2026 by Capstone.
All rights reserved. No part of this publication may be reproduced in whole or in part, or stored in a retrieval system, or transmitted in any form or by any means, electronic, mechanical, photocopying, recording, or otherwise, without written permission of the publisher.

Library of Congress Cataloging-in-Publication Data is available on the Library of Congress website.

ISBN: 9798875227066 (hardback)
ISBN: 9798875230011 (paperback)
ISBN: 9798875229992 (eBook PDF)

Image Credits: iStock: DOUGBERRY, cover, Hispanolistic, 14–15, Image Source, 8, Jasonfang, 10–11, Nelson Gaspar, 21, THEPALMER, 1, 17, underworld111, 18, Wildroze, 19, Wirestock, 20; Shutterstock: elena moiseeva, 22–23, Erickson Stock, 6–7, FotoDuets, 2–3, Jeff Thrower, 9, 24, LightField Studios, 4–5, Monkey Business Images, 16, Roman Babakin, 12–13